PLANET MOUSE

Written by Billy Treacy
Illustrated by Richard Watson

OXFORD
UNIVERSITY PRESS

Words to look out for …

assist *VERB*
To assist someone is to help them, usually in a practical way.

benefit *VERB*
You benefit from something, or it benefits you, when it helps you.

manage *VERB*
To manage something is to be able to do it although it is difficult.

monitor *NOUN*
a computer or television screen

routine *NOUN*
a regular or fixed way of doing things

sample *NOUN*
a small amount that shows what something is like

Chapter 1

For a long time, Hana didn't know her mouse was an alien.

In many ways, Agi was like any other mouse. He had a normal mouse routine. He got up at night. He ran in his wheel. He ate lots of mouse food.

A routine is a regular or fixed way of doing things.

3

However, Agi sometimes acted very strangely. Whenever he escaped from his cage, he didn't behave like a regular mouse.

Hana once spotted Agi looking up at the stars. He was looking at them fondly, as if he remembered them.

One night, something very strange indeed happened. Hana saw Agi crawl out from a hole in the wall. She was sure she had closed the cage door.

When Hana called out his name, Agi scurried back inside the cage. Even more strange, she watched him fasten the door himself.

Then there was the night Agi spoke.

"Hello, Hana!" said a little voice.

Hana sat up and stared into Agi's cage.

Agi stared back. Then he waved!

"It's me, your pet mouse," he said.

Hana did not know what to say to this. What are you supposed to say when your pet suddenly talks?

Agi peered through the bars. "Are you there? My eyes aren't the best these days."

"I am," said Hana. She couldn't believe she was talking to a mouse!

"Good. I need you to assist me," Agi announced.

"Would you like some more water?" Hana asked. "Or perhaps some food?"

To assist someone is to help them, usually in a practical way.

Agi shook his head.
"No, no. I need your help to get back to my home planet."

"You're ... an *alien*?" said Hana.

"Of course I'm an alien," said Agi, rolling his eyes. "I'm a talking mouse!"

He made his way to the hole in the wall. Hana followed him.

"I don't think I can fit through that," she said.

"Indeed," said Agi.

All of a sudden, there was a loud clunk. The wall hissed open. It revealed a giant copy of the wheel in his cage.

"This is my spacewheel," said Agi. "It's big enough for you to fit inside."

Hana stepped into the wheel and sat down. Monitors flashed on either side of her, showing lots of charts and measurements.

It was hard for Hana to know what to look at first.

A monitor is a computer or television screen.

"Don't worry, Hana," Agi said kindly. "You're in safe paws."

Agi pressed a green button, which caused a very loud sound. Then the wall in front of them slid open. Shining before them were the bright lights of the city.

Hana was glad her parents were fast asleep.

11

"Hana," said Agi. "I'm going to press the planetary propeller thrust button. Do you know what that means?"

"Not a clue," admitted Hana. There was no point pretending she understood. "What does the propeller thingy do?"

"It will send us into space," explained Agi. "In which case, you'd benefit from a seatbelt!"

"Oh, right!" said Hana. She strapped herself in.

Agi put his seatbelt on too. "Right! Time to get moving," he said.

He swung round in his chair and pressed a big square button.

You benefit from something, or it benefits you, when it helps you.

Chapter 2

The spacewheel roared into action. Before Hana knew it, they were flying over the street below.

The city lights grew tiny as they hurtled upwards. Soon they were surrounded by the brightness of stars.

"It's beautiful," whispered Hana.

Agi's whiskers twitched. "This is just a sample of what's to come!"

A sample is a small amount that shows what something is like.

As they shot upwards, the world beneath them became smaller.

Soon, the city was just a splash of light. Hana saw her entire country laid out beneath her.

Agi pressed another button. "Let's speed this up," he said.

The spacewheel zoomed so fast that Hana felt dizzy. Soon, the Earth looked no bigger than a marble. It shone in a sea of stars.

"Wonderful, isn't it?" said Agi.

Hana nodded. Her world looked so small and peaceful.

Hana suddenly felt sad. She realized she was very far from her family and friends.

"Everyone I know lives on that little planet," she said with a sigh.

"Everyone you know *so far*," Agi corrected her. "There are plenty of friends to make up here. I'll show you."

Agi took Hana's hand in his paw. "Years ago, I often visited your planet on special trips," he explained. "One of my tasks was to collect food samples, but then I met you. Now it's time for me to say goodbye to Earth."

"I need you to help me find Planet Mouse, my home," he said.

A sample is a small amount that shows what something is like.

Suddenly, two objects sped towards them. They looked like harmless cardboard boxes at first. As they got closer, Hana saw two creatures inside them.

"What are those?" asked Hana.

Agi's eyes had widened in fear.

"Space cats!" shouted Agi. "We need to get out of here!" He began pressing lots of buttons.

"There are cats in space?" asked Hana.

"Of course! They chase space mice, after all!" said Agi.

Hana looked closer. The cats had glowing green eyes. One of them licked its lips.

Agi moved faster than Hana had ever seen him move. The monitor flashed an angry red sign.

"I'm going to fly us through a field of enormous rocks," Agi said. "Those cats are on our tails!"

"I don't have a tail!" joked Hana.

A monitor is a computer or television screen

21

The spaceship rolled left and right, dodging one rock after another.

Hana kept an eye on their speed. "I think we've managed to escape the cats," she said.

They shared a sigh of relief.

To manage something is to be able to do it although it is difficult.

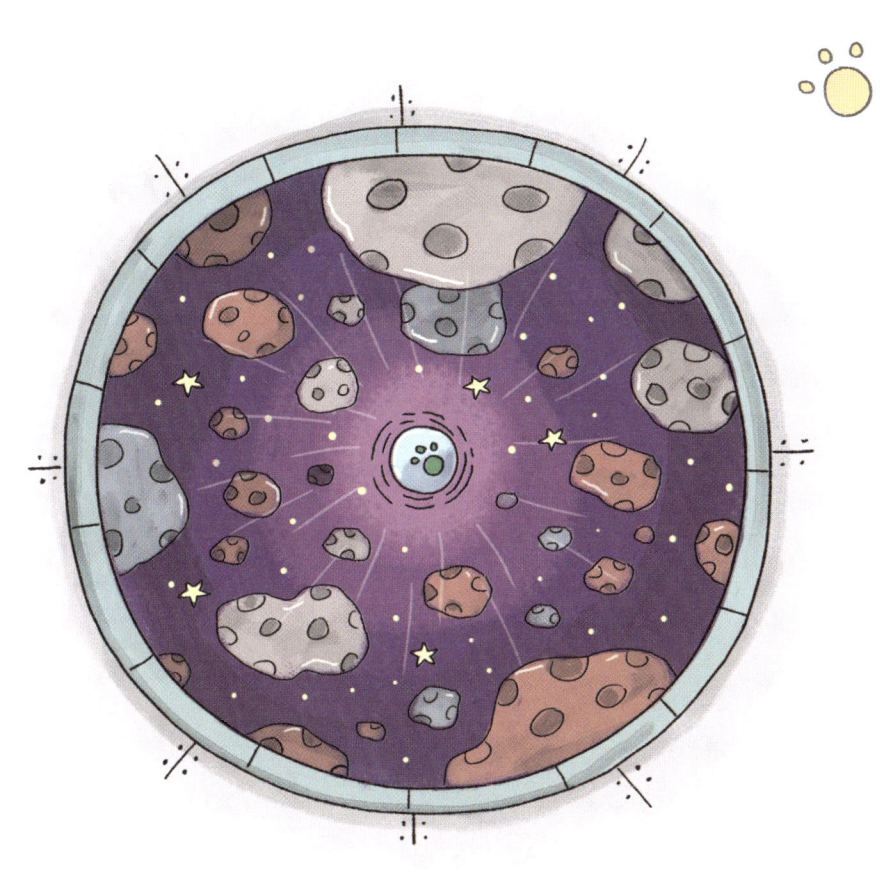

Slowly, a small planet came into view through one of the windows. Hana gasped.

"What is it?" asked Agi.

The land on the planet was shaped like a giant paw print.

"I can see Planet Mouse!" said Hana excitedly. "Steer this way!"

Soon she could see lights coming from tiny mouse cities.

Agi wiped away a tear of joy. "I'm home," he said. He looked up at Hana. "Will you help me land the spaceship?"

Hana smiled and nodded. There was nothing she wanted to do more!

Chapter 3

The spacewheel slowly sank through the clouds of Planet Mouse.

A city slowly came into view. It looked like all the dollhouses and model railways on Earth put together. At the heart of the city were some tall buildings. They reminded Hana of the cardboard tubes she collected for Agi.

The spacewheel landed smoothly.

Agi's world was just like Hana's, but smaller. Everywhere she looked, mice were scampering about.

However, Hana towered over everything. She was taller than the highest building! She didn't belong here.

"Now I understand how you felt on Earth," she said. "This world is not built for me."

Just then, the mice stopped and looked up in shock.

"I'm not here to hurt anyone!" said Hana.

"It's not just you they're scared of," said Agi. "Look behind you!"

Hana turned around. Hovering above them were the two space cats! Their green eyes glowed.

The mice darted for shelter. They disappeared into their homes and looked out through the windows.

When the cats landed, they began to prowl the city.

Hana tried to make herself look even bigger. She puffed out her chest.

"Leave these mice alone!" she yelled.

The cats walked over. Their eyes were fixed on Hana. Then, they rolled on to their backs.

"They don't want to eat us," said Agi. "They want to play with *you*!"

Hana crouched down and stroked the cats' tummies. They purred happily.

"It seems these cats will be happy to take you home," said Agi.

Hana laughed, but not for long. "Does that mean you're not coming with me?" she said.

"I'm afraid not," Agi said sadly, "but I will never forget you, Hana. I will treasure my memories of eating food from your hand. Thank you for assisting me."

To assist someone is to help them, usually in a practical way.

Chapter 4

Back at home, Pop came and placed his arms around Hana.

"It's always hard saying goodbye to a pet," he said. "Agi was lucky to have enjoyed his time with you."

Hana glanced out of the window at the night sky.

"Wherever Agi is now, I'm sure he wants you to be happy," said Pop.

Hana thought about how glad Agi had been to go home. "Don't worry," she smiled. "I know."